1 Introduction

At the onset of the financial crisis in the summer of 2007, short-term funding markets experienced a severe disruption: securitization markets—in particular the market for asset-backed commercial paper—collapsed and interbank markets froze (Strahan, 2008; Brunnermeier, 2009). Although conditions improved in early 2008 relative to late 2007 due to an aggressive policy response and a massive liquidity injection into the banking sector, funding markets experienced significant distress again during the fall of 2008 after Lehman Brothers and AIG failed, and Fannie Mae and Freddie Mac were placed under conservatorship. As Gorton (2009) argues, the financial crisis resembled a banking panic that took the form of a run of financial firms on other financial firms. The panic centered on the repurchase agreement (repo) market, which suffered a run when lenders withdrew their funds by declining to roll over their loan agreements, and by raising their repo haircuts. Concerned about the size and location of the exposure to subprime-related assets, banks stopped lending to other banks, and decided to hoard liquid buffers in response to several factors: widespread concerns about the solvency of their counterparties in interbank operations, increased risks in their asset portfolios, and potential liquidity risk arising from draw-downs of committed lines of credit.

This paper studies the main determinants of bank liquidity hoarding and its effects on bank lending during the recent financial crisis. I propose a measure of liquidity risk—unrealized losses on securities holdings—that accounts for the severe exposure of banks to potential capital losses at the peak of the run in the repo market and that describes the precautionary motive for hoarding liquid asset s. Unrealized losses in securities holdings represent the write-downs of securities (a large portion of which are used as collateral in repo transactions) that result from mark-to-market accounting of investment portfolios. In other words, they reflect the exposure to future capital losses for banks if they had to sell those assets at fire sale prices. This source of liquidity risk has not been explored at length in the literature, due perhaps to the lack of reliable data on repo market transactions and the few balance sheet items related to credit exposure covered by collateral in those transactions.

Liquidity management decisions are not uniform across banks, as they depend on the nature of the risks being faced. I document how liquidity hoarding became manifest at the onset and during the peak of the crisis by examining the behavior of various assets commonly included in the definition of liquid assets. Depending on the type of funding pressures they faced, I find that banks sold assets worth selling, such as treasuries and government securities, because the return on those assets was almost zero. Banks accumulated cash and excess reserves at the central bank because of the interest earned on reserve balances. Banks also accumulated securities such as mortgage-backed securities (MBS) issued or guaranteed by Government-Sponsored Enterprises (GSEs), such as Fannie Mae and Freddie Mac. These securities had a positive return due to an implicit government guarantee and provided valuation gains that partly compensated for the losses generated by subprime mortgage-related securities.

Previous work finds that a measure of off-balance sheet liquidity risk for commercial banks, such as the fraction of unused loan commitments to their lending capacity, is a key determinant of bank liquidy management. In particular, Cornett, McNutt, Strahan, and Tehranian (2011), emphasize that large undrawn loan commitments expose banks to sudden liquidity demand from corporations. That risk materialized during the financial crisis, as firms in need of liquidity rushed to draw down funds from their committed credit lines and forced banks to build up liquidity buffers to meet such increased demand. These drawdowns displaced banks' lending capacity and constrained their new credit origination. Despite the significance of this result, I argue that an important part of the story during the recent financial crisis is still missing.

I extend the work of Cornett, McNutt, Strahan, and Tehranian (2011) in four ways. First, I show that during the financial crisis banks increased their holdings of liquid assets also in anticipation of future losses from securities write-downs (measured by unrealized securities losses) and expected loan losses (measured by loan loss reserves). Furthermore, unrealized securities losses and loan loss reserves seem to better capture the risks stemming from banks' asset management and provide supporting evidence for the precautionary nature of liquidity hoarding. Second, as noted above, I study the heterogeneity across different categories of liquid assets. Since asset categories are moving in opposite directions, each must be examined in tandem to understand the nature of liquidity hoarding. Third, my results also indicate that liquidity hoarding occurred across all banking institutions regardless of their size. I show that the drawdown of unused commitments occured at the time when banks—in particular the larger ones—were hit by large securities and loan losses. This result suggests that corporations rushed to their banks to draw their credit lines concerned about the liquidity and solvency of the banking sector, as pointed out by Ivashina and Scharfstein (2010). Lastly, I examine the behavior of very large banks (with total assets above $50 billion) during the financial crisis. I show that, in addition to liquidity risk from loan commitments and securities losses, these banks were exposed to the l iquidity risk emanating from drawdowns of liquidity backup lines to their conduits used in loan securitizations.

Bank liquidity hoarding is not a new phenomenon. For example, in the aftermath of the Great Depression, and particularly during the late 1930s, U.S. commercial banks accumulated substantial amounts of voluntary excess reserves. As Ramos (1996) points out, during and immediately after a severe liquidity crisis, banks hoard excess cash to self-insure against further drains of cash and to send markets a strong message that their solvency is not at risk and that bank runs are not justifiable.[1] The situation during the banking crisis of the 1930s clearly resembles the bank behavior during the most recent financial crisis. As suggested at that time, banks sought to build up liquidity buffers to reduce their risk exposure on the asset side of their balance sheets at times when capital and debt was very expensive.

As previous work suggests, in managing their liquidity, banks take into account the stability of their funding sources such as equity capital and deposits.[2] My findings indicate that bank capital and deposits are important for both large and small banks, though they seem to be more relevant for small banks. This result is consistent with the view that core deposits are a more important source of funding for smaller banks, given that small banks generally have more restricted access to interbank markets and the central bank's discount window. Core deposits represented an important funding source to increase the holdings of government securities and MBS of small banks.

---

[1] During the 1930s banks were required to increase the level of reserves as a fraction of their deposits. The argument in Ramos (1996) is that banks responded by accumulating large amounts of voluntary reserves, that is, reserves beyond the policy requirement.

[2] Berger and Bouwman (2009) show that bank capital is a key determinant for liquidity creation. They also present evidence that liquidity creation varies by bank size. Consistent with these findings, my results show that capital played a significant role in the increased holdings of liquid assets during the financial crisis.

Regarding the role of deposits as a stable source of funds that adds to the accumulation of liquid buffers, I find supporting evidence of a flight-to-quality effect in deposits within the banking sector. My findings suggest that non-core deposits flew out of banks and returned in the form of core deposits, first to hoarding banks and later to non-hoarding banks. Therefore, I provide evidence of inflows of core deposits at the onset of the crisis to banks that chose to hoard liquidity. During the first year of the crisis, banks highly exposed to securities losses sought to hoard liquid assets as a war chest against future losses. As the crisis deepened during the fall of 2008, exposed banks lost confidence and their core deposits flowed into less exposed banks (non-hoarders of liquidity). In line with earlier effects of disruptions in interbank markets, my results suggest that the same factors leading to precautionary liquidity hoarding also contributed to the sharp decline in bank lending. I find that for liquidity-hoarding banks, more than one-fourth of the lending contraction is due to the precautionary motive.

The results presented here also have important policy implications. As the recent financial crisis demonstrates, liquidity hoarding affects the normal functioning of short-term funding markets. Due to increased uncertainty and the fear of prolonged restrictions to accessing interbank loans, banks that choose to hoard liquidity may cause a rise in borrowing costs that has an adverse impact on less liquid banks. Moreover, if liquidity-hoarding banks have sufficient market power to manipulate asset prices, some form of predatory behavior may arise. Acharya, Gromb, and Yorulmazer (2008) suggest that liquid banks under-provide liquidity so as to benefit from the fire sale of assets from illiquid banks in desperate need of liquid funds. Hence, liquidity hoarding by banks may constrain the effectiveness of monetary policy that is aimed at restoring the stability of funding markets. Moreover, the considerable fear associated with the riskiness of banks' portfolios further limits the ability of policy actions to revamp credit growth and stimulate the real economy. Finally, the paper also highlights important differences in the distribution of liquid assets across banks depending on their size. Understanding such differences is crucial in the context of a regulatory reform and must be taken into account in the implementation of capital and liquidity requirements (such as the proposed liquidity coverage ratio and the net stable funding ratio) for banking institutions.

The remainder of the paper is organized as follows. Section 2 briefly describes the related literature and discusses how my empirical results compare with previous findings. In Section 3, I document the events associated with the disruption in short-term funding markets leading to the hoarding of bank liquidity. I also review the policy tools used to deal with the financial crisis and the way liquidity hoarding manifested itself in the banking sector. Section 4 provides the empirical results for the determinants and the main implications of bank liquidity hoarding. Section 5 concludes.

2 Related Literature

Several theoretical papers have examined the motivation for banks to hoard liquid assets. For example, banks may decide to hoard liquidity for precautionary reasons if they believe they will be unable to obtain interbank loans when they are affected by temporary liquidity shortages (Allen and Gale, 2004). Precautionary liquidity hoarding has also been modeled as the response of banks to the fear of forced asset liquidation, as in the frameworks of Diamond and Rajan (2009), Gale and Yorulmazer (2011). In Diamond and Rajan (2009) banks hoard liquidity in anticipation of future liquidation of assets which, in the context of severe disruptions in funding markets, provide a high expected return from holding cash. In the model of Gale and Yorulmazer, banks hoard liquidity to protect themselves against future liquidity shocks (precautionary motive) or to take advantage of potential sales (strategic motive). Acharya and Skeie (2011) develop a model in which banks hoard liquidity in anticipation of insolvency of their counterparties in interbank markets (rollover risk).

Another strand of the literature derives liquidity hoarding as a result of Knightian uncertainty when due to increased uncertainty banks make decisions based on worst-case scenarios (Caballero and Krishnamurthy, 2008)—and contagion in financial networks. For example, Caballero and Simsek (2009) propose a framework in which banks operate in complex network structures. In those market structures, the information that banks normally collect to assess the financial conditions of their trading partners becomes insufficient. To learn more about their counterparty risks, they have to collect information on the health of the trading partners of the trading partners of the trading partners, and so on. During times of financial distress, this process becomes extremely costly. Moreover, the confusion and uncertainty that follows a liquidity shock can trigger massive flight-to-quality episodes, and force illiquid banks to withdraw from loan commitments and illiquid positions. As the flight-to-quality unfolds, the financial crisis spreads.

In a similar vein, Zawadowski (2011) uses the idea of financial contagion in network structures to show that uncertainty in short-term funding markets among interconnected institutions can lead to excessive liquidity hoarding. The author shows that, after a liquidity shock, uncertainty about not being able to roll over interbank loans leads to inefficient liquidation of assets, which causes no default in equilibrium but a significant drop in lending. The novelty in his analysis is that uncertainty is capable of spreading and magnifying the impact of liquidity shocks through an interbank network. This network works as an interwoven structure in which each bank finances several other banks, so that uncertainty about funding in one bank spreads to more and more banks in the consecutive layers of intermediation.

Recent empirical evidence on liquidity hoarding is provided by Acharya and Merrouche (2010), Heider, Hoerova, and Holthausen (2008), De Haan and Van den End (2011), and Wolman and Ennis (2011). Using data for large settlement banks in the U.K., Acharya and Merrouche (2011) show that banks significantly increased their liquidity buffers after August 2007. This increase in liquid assets occurred when the interbank markets started to dry up and bank borrowing costs ballooned. Heider, Hoerova and Holthausen (2008) also provide evidence of liquidity hoarding in the euro interbank market. Unlike the very small spreads and infinitesimal amounts of excess reserves in normal times, they show that the unsecured euro interbank market exhibited significantly higher spreads leading to a dramatic increase in banks' excess reserves. Using a panel Vector Autoregression (p-VAR) approach, De Haan and Van den End (2011) find that in response to funding liquidity shocks, Dutch banks reduce wholesale lending, hoard liquidity in the form of liquid bonds and central bank reserves, and conduct fire sales of equity securities. Finally, Wolman and Ennis (2011) using data on U.S. commercial banks find that banks holding large excess reserves at the Federal Reserve since the fall of 2008 also increased their holdings of other liquid assets such as short-term securities. Furthermore, their findings indicate that banks holding high levels of liquidity have enough capital to expand their lending without facing binding capital requirements.

3 Liquidity Hoarding During the Financial Crisis

This section briefly describes the events associated with the financial turmoil of 2007-2009. It also reviews the changes to monetary aggregates associated with the quick and aggressive response of the Treasury and the Federal Reserve to the financial crisis through numerous liquidity provision programs and relates these policy actions to changes in commercial banks' assets.

3.1 Disruption in Short-term Funding Markets

The financial crisis started in August 2007 when interbank markets froze and the market for asset-backed commercial paper (ABCP) collapsed. As shown in the upper panel of Figure 1, outstanding volumes in the ABCP market shrunk by about $350 billion in the fall of 2007 (from $1.2 trillion in August to about $850 billion by year-end). The dry-up of liquidity continued in 2008 as investors became concerned about the credit quality and the liquidation value of collateral backing ABCP transactions (see Covitz, Liang, and Suarez, 2011). Similarly, outstanding volumes in the unsecured commercial paper market for financial firms—relatively unaffected by the freeze in interbank markets in 2007—plunged by about $350 billion after the failure of Lehman Brothers and the bailout of AIG in October 2008.

In the face of fear and uncertainty in financial markets, large institutional investors withdrew their funds from the collective pool of cash by declining to roll over their loan agreements. In normal times, this can be done without causing significant effects on interest rates. However, with deepening concerns about the credit quality of counterparties and the fact that the magnitude of the exposure to subprime-related assets was unknown, investors withdrew their funds en masse. This withdrawal created a huge shortage of collateral, which forced institutions to sell securities to meet the increased demand for liquidity. As the repo and interbank markets shrunk, the increased sale of securities drove their prices further down. Such deterioration in the value of securities (most of which were being used as collateral in repo transactions) was a natural source of liquidity risk leading to the precautionary hoarding of liquid assets, as shown by an aggregate measure of liquidity (the share of liquid assets to total assets) in the lower panel of Figure 1.

Figure 2 depicts the aggregate amount of (unrealized) securities losses for the banking sector between 2005:Q1 and 2009:Q2. After falling from about $40 billion in mid-2006 to less than $10 billion over the second half of 2007, unrealized losses increased again during 2008.[3] As financial strains intensified in the fall of 2008, securities losses reached a peak of $52 billion at the height of the financial crisis, in October 2008. Large banks were more severely hit by securities losses than other bank-size groups. For example, the largest 10 banks held about 45 percent of the available-for-sale securities in investment accounts and accounted for two-thirds of the securities losses during 2008.[4] As shown in the next section, although securities losses had a bigger impact on large banking institutions, they were a widespread problem for all banks, and medium and small banks were not immune.

3.2 Liquidity Programs and the Federal Reserve response to the crisis

In an effort to ease conditions in interbank and credit markets, the Federal Reserve provided a significant amount of liquidity to the banking sector via several new facilities.[5] Credit extended through lending facilities totaled $1600 billion in 2008 and $250 billion in 2009. Excluding liquidity swaps with other central banks and credit extended to specific institutions such as Bear Stearns and AIG through asset purchases (portfolio holdings of Maiden Lane LLC), the Federal Reserve expanded liquidity by about $600 billion over 2008, with most liquidity extended in the last two quarters of 2008 when financial and economic conditions deteriorated sharply.[6] As a result of this aggressive response to the credit crisis, the Federal Reserve's balance sheet increased from about $1 trillion in the summer of 2007 to about $2.2 trillion by the end of 2009.

---

[3] Part of the decline towards the end of 2007 may be explained by some reclassification of certain types of securities out of investment accounts and into trading accounts. This shift occurred after some banks, mainly large institutions, adopted new rules on fair value accounting (e.g. FAS 159 on fair value option). Banks that elected the fair value option had incentives to reclassify their securities, as unrealized losses on those securities were not reported in current earnings.

[4] See Profits and Balance Sheet Developments at U.S. Commercial Banks in 2008, Federal Reserve Bulletin 2009.

[5] These new facilities include the Money Market Investor Funding Facility (MMIFF), the Asset-Backed Commercial Paper Money Market Mutual Fund Liquidity Facility (AMLF), the Commercial Paper Funding Facility (CPFF), the Primary Dealer Credit Facility (PDCF), the Term Securities Lending Facility (TSLF), and the temporary liquidity swap arrangements between the Federal Reserve and foreign central banks.

[6] This number corresponds to the flow of total borrowing of depository institutions from the Federal Reserve during 2008. Total borrowing from the Federal Reserve is equal to the term auction credit plus other loans. For comparison, as of year-end 2007, the term auction credit and other loans equaled $40 billion and $5 billion, respectively.

As the functioning of financial markets improved, many of the liquidity programs expired or were closed in 2009. The composition of the Federal Reserve's balance sheet continued to shift in the second half of 2009 and early 2010, when the liquidity support to markets took the form of purchases of Treasuries and mortgage-backed securities. The considerable decline in the credit extended through the various liquidity programs was more than offset by the increase in securities holdings.

Combined with an approximately $220 billion capital injection through the Capital Purchase Program (TARP), a total of about $820 billion was provided to the banking industry during 2008 and 2009. Interestingly, most of the funds received by banks resulted in an increase in excess reserves of $765 billion over 2008 and $318 billion in 2009. This information suggests that banks decided to keep the injected funds in the form of reserves at the central bank.

The buildup of excess reserves held at the central bank during the implementation of the liquidity programs provides the first piece of evidence of liquidity hoarding in the United States. Moreover, this evidence is consistent with the argument that injecting more excess reserves into the banking sector does not necessarily lead to more bank lending. As Martin, McAndrews, and Skeie (2011) argue, in the context of interest paid on bank reserves and no binding reserve requirements, excess reserves may end up contracting lending. This is the case when interest rates are very low (almost zero) so that the marginal return on loans is smaller than the opportunity cost of making a loan. The adverse effect on lending is more apparent when banks face increased balance sheet costs associated with agency costs or regulatory requirements for capital or leverage ratios. Using a related argument, Hancock and Passmore (2011) contend that when the cost of capital is high and banks are capital constrained, additional excess reserves impose a tax on the banking sector because they tie up capital for a low profit (or unprofitable) use. As mentioned above, a large accumulation of excess reserves at the central bank after monetary expansions is also found using data for settlement banks in the U.K. and the unsecured euro interbank market.

3.3 Commercial Banks' Balance Sheet data

Figure 3 depicts the changes in the composition of bank assets in 2008 and 2009. By far the most striking change in aggregate commercial bank balance-sheet conditions occurred in the holdings of safe and liquid assets. Holdings of cash and securities (both treasuries and agency) increased $869 billion over 2008 and 2009 ($375 billion and $494 billion, respectively). Since most of the Federal Reserve's liquidity programs—such as the Term Auction Facility and the Asset-Backed Commercial Paper Money Market Mutual Fund Liquidity Facility (AMLF)—were specifically designed to foster the normal functioning of particular financial markets, it is not entirely surprising that the increase in securities holdings by commercial banks is explained by the liquidity provision of these specific programs. Indeed, the observed expansion of securities holdings may reflect the successful propping up of liquidity in specific short-term funding markets.

The sharp increase in the holdings of liquid assets contrasts with the evolution of bank loans during these years, especially C&I loans which declined $211 billion. In other words, the aggregate bank balance-sheet information and monetary aggregate figures seem to suggest that the majority of the funds that have been injected into banking organizations did not result directly in additional lending.[7] Instead, banks chose to hoard these liquidity and capital provisions to build up a cushion to protect against further capital losses and expected write-downs.[8] Another manifestation of the liquidity pressures banks faced during the crisis is the large reduction in trading assets and fed funds sold to non-bank institutions (decline in other assets of $449 billion).

Regarding the liability side of their balance sheets, most of the counterpart changes in liquid assets over 2008 and 2009 were also explained by a significant increase in bank deposits. Despite the slowdown in deposit growth in 2007, banks experienced significant deposit inflows from investors

---

[7] It is possible that some mortgage credit provision occurred through the sale of mortgage loans to GSEs for which banks received MBS in return.

[8] Banks were lending a very small portion of the funds injected into the sector. Although the Federal Reserve's liquidity programs and the Treasury's TARP capital injections both share the broader objective of preserving financial stability during times of financial turmoil, the direct emphasis of the two policies on bank lending are different. In particular, the TARP's capital purchase program (CPP) was specifically intended for banks to lend the capital received. In contrast, most of the liquidity programs set up by the Federal Reserve were not directly aimed at reviving bank lending, although they did—by improving the functioning of specific markets—aim to ultimately contribute to greater credit availability for businesses and households. Thus, one might still expect these liquidity programs to reinforce the objectives of TARP and increase somewhat banks' willingness to extend loans.

pulling their funds from money market mutual funds, particularly during the fall of 2008 and after the failure of Lehman Brothers and AIG. As will be seen in section 4, the deposit expansion was not uniform across banks and had a significant influence on the decision to hoard liquidity.

4 Empirical Analysis

4.1 Data and Methodology

I construct a panel dataset using quarterly balance sheet data from the Reports of Income and Condition (Call Reports) for all U.S. commercial banks between 2005 and 2009. Data are aggregated at the Bank Holding Company level to deal with common ownership of bank subsidiaries. I compute ratios and growth rates for assets, liabilities, and some off-balance sheet operations such as unused loan commitments. To deal with mergers and acquisitions, I drop bank observations with asset growth greater than 10 percent and winsorize variables at the 1st and 99th percentiles. The remaining sample consists of 109,494 bank-quarter observations for approximately 7,500 institutions.

Liquidity hoarders in this study are defined as banks for which the average ratio of total liquid assets to total assets increased by more than 3 percentage points from a period before the crisis (2005:Q1 to 2007:Q4) to the crisis period (2008:Q1 to 2009:Q2).[9] All other banks are defined as non-hoarders. This definition excludes, for example, banks which for operational purposes are highly liquid before and during the financial crisis. Total liquid assets are calculated as the sum of cash (including balances at other banks and reserves at the central bank), fed funds (including reverse repos), and investment securities (including MBS, asset-backed securities (ABS), and government securities).

Table 1 presents descriptive statistics (means) for both liquidity hoarders and non-hoarders before and during the financial crisis. Liquidity hoarders reduce their lending much more than non-hoarders during the crisis (loan growth is considerably smaller for liquidity hoarders). On average,

---

[9]Although arbitrary, the 3-percentage-point cutoff identifies about one-sixth of the banks in the sample as being liquidity hoarders. I also utilize 2.5 and 3.5 percentage point cutoffs and obtain similar results.

the annualized growth rate of loans for liquidity hoarders dropped 5.2 percentage points (from 4.9 percent before the crisis to negative 0.3 percent during the crisis), almost three times the decline in annual growth of their non-hoarding counterparts (2.2 percentage points). Furthermore, liquidity hoarders seem to be slightly larger and better capitalized than their non-hoarding counterparts, both before and during the crisis period. Differences in almost all variables across groups before the crisis and during the crisis are statistically significant at the 1 percent level.

Figure 4 presents the evolution of the ratio of total liquid assets to total assets for the average commercial bank in the U.S. between 2005 and 2009, as well as the share of some of its components: cash and fed funds, government securities (including Treasuries), and agency MBS (MBS issued or guaranteed by GSEs, which investors perceive as having an implicit government guarantee). The striking insight from Figure 4 is the remarkable gap in the behavior of liquid assets across asset categories between liquidity-hoarding banks and their non-hoarding counterparts. Such disparity confirms that the disposition to hold liquid assets is not uniform across banks or across asset categories, and highlights the advantage of exploiting bank-level variation to study the nature of liquidity hoarding. The difference in the liquid assets ratio across the two groups of banks widens considerably (from 10 to 12 percentage points) between 2008:Q3 and 2009:Q1, precisely the period when the financial crisis intensified.

In October 2008, after the failure of Lehman Brothers, the conservatorship of Fannie Mae and Freddie Mac, and the AIG bailout, a measure of counterparty risk in interbank markets such as the TED spread (difference in yield between LIBOR and a Treasury Bill of similar maturity) moved up to a record level of 430 basis points. Among the liquid asset categories on the balance sheet, banks started hoarding cash (including fed funds) and agency MBS during the crisis. The holding of government securities, however, declined after the third quarter of 2007, especially for non-hoarding banks. This decline suggests that banks were selling treasuries and other government securities to cope with increased funding pressures. Since asset categories are moving in opposite directions, each must be examined in tandem to understand the nature of liquidity hoarding.

4.2 Measures of Liquidity Risk

To investigate the causes of liquidity hoarding, I use a regression framework similar to that in Cornett, McNutt, Strahan, and Tehranian (2011). The regression analysis considers the share of liquid assets in total assets as the dependent variable, expressed as changes normalized by total assets. Potential explanatory variables include the log of total assets (a proxy for bank size), the Tier 1 capital ratio, the share of core deposits (the sum of transaction deposits and other insured deposits) in total assets (a proxy for the role of stable sources of funding), and the unused commitment ratio, measured by the share of unused commitments to lending capacity—unused commitments plus assets—(a proxy for off-balance sheet funding liquidity stemming from loans).

I hypothesize that the precautionary motive to hoard liquidity is better approximated by a liquidity risk measure that captures a bank's exposure to expected losses in their securities portfolio (security write-downs) in anticipation of future liquidation of assets, as in Diamond and Rajan (2009). I also propose a measure of credit risk given by the share of loan loss reserves in total loans to control for the possibility that further deterioration in credit quality forces banks to reallocate their assets from risky loans to safe and liquid securities. Unlike traditional measures of credit quality, such as net charge-offs and delinquent loans, loan loss reserves have a forward-looking component that reflects banks' efforts to increase their loan provisioning in anticipation of expected losses, and therefore, provide another motivation to hoard cash in anticipation of such losses. My proposed risk measures are therefore: the ratio of securities losses (unrealized losses on available-for-sale securities) to available for sale securities and the ratio of loan reserves (allowance for loan losses) to total loans. I add these two measures as key explanatory variables in the regression equation of liquid assets.

I use both gross and net (of taxes) measures of unrealized gains (losses) in available-for-sale securities. Net unrealized gains (losses) are obtained directly from the regulatory capital schedule (RC-R) of Call Reports (RCFD-8434), whereas gross unrealized gains (losses) are computed as the difference between the amortized cost and the fair value of available-for-sale securities as reported in the securities schedule (RC-B) of Call Reports. The amortized cost of securities is their book value (acquisition cost) adjusted for the discount or premium paid at purchase. The difference between amortized cost and fair value is the change in market value (write-up or write-down) of the securities still being held on banks' investment portfolios.[10]

My proposed measure of liquidity risk is naturally linked to the fear and uncertainty surrounding the disruptions in short-term funding markets for banks: the repo (collateralized funding) and the interbank markets (uncollateralized funding). In particular, the repo market provided a key source of funds to dealer and commercial banks actively engaged in trading structured products in the months prior to the panic of 2007.

As Acharya and Merrouche (2010) argue, the drying up of short-term liquidity markets caused a significant increase in borrowing rates for all banks, regardless of counterparty risk. The spike in funding costs suggests an interest rate contagion channel through the interbank markets, which is well described by rate spreads such as the TED spread (3-month LIBOR rate minus 3-month Treasury rate) or the LIBOR-OIS spread (LIBOR rate over the corresponding overnight index swap rate). As in Cornett, McNutt, Strahan, and Tehranian (2011), I include interaction terms of the TED spread with the key explanatory variables as the main focus of the analysis.

4.3 Econometric Results

In contrast to Cornett, McNutt, Strahan, and Tehranian and as suggested by Figure 4, I investigate the main determinants of liquidity hoarding for different asset categories.[11] My regression estimates are shown in table 2. The first two columns in table 2 are included as a reference, as they replicate the findings of Cornett, McNutt, Strahan, and Tehranian (2011), who examined an overall measure

---

[10] Unrealized securities losses are reported with a negative sign (a positive sign then indicates a security gain). For the ease of interpretation, I switch the sign and take a positive sign as indicative of a loss.

[11] My definition of liquid assets includes mortgage-backed securities. Cornett, McNutt, Strahan, and Tehranian considered that all MBS and ABS became illiquid during the crisis, and therefore dropped them from their definition of liquid assets. Their rationale was that these securities would be held due to their inability to be sold or used as collateral in rolling over short-term funding after the collapse of the market for securitized assets. However, most of these securitized assets are comprised of agency MBS. With and implicit government guarantee, it is not entirely clear that the majority of these securities should be excluded and considered illiquid as their market value was not really impaired during the collapse of the funding and securitization markets. In fact, most of the securities losses in banks' balance sheets result from the write downs of ABS and non-agency MBS. As shown in Figure 4, agency MBS represents a large fraction of the liquid assets that banks were hoarding.

of liquid assets to total assets. As can be seen, unused commitments appear to be a significant determinant of increased liquidity buffers mesured by the overall liquid asset ratio, and the ratio of cash, fed funds and reverse repos to total assets.[12] Columns 3 through 6 show my estimates by type of liquid assets. My main findings are: (1) as documented in prior work, stable sources of funding such as deposits and capital are key determinants of the holdings of liquid assets. Consistent with Cornett, McNutt, Strahan and Tehranian (2011), I find that core deposits substitute for cash and fed funds as banks use these stable funding sources to fund loans and commitments. Holdings of liquid assets also decrease with bank capital; (2) Although table 1 suggests that liquidity hoarders appear to be slightly larger than non-hoarders, the regression results do not support the hypothesis that larger banks hoard more liquid assets. On the contrary the results indicate that the holdings of liquid assets decrease with bank size;[13] (3) My proposed measures of on-balance sheet risk, unrealized securities losses and loan loss reserves, play a significant role, and seem to complement off-balance sheet liquidity risk stemming from the possibility of increased drawdown demand for committed loans.

When looking at each individual component of the overall liquid asset ratio such as cash and fed funds, government securities, and agency MBS (columns 4 through 6, respectively) my results suggest that this complementarity between on-balance sheet and off-balance sheet risks is particularly important to explain the hoarding of cash and fed funds during times of financial distress. However, that is not the case for the holdings of government securities and agency MBS. Columns 5 and 6 indicate that, in general, large unused commitments seem to reduce the holdings of government securities and to increase the holdings of agency MBS. However, they seem to act in the opposite direction during times of financial distress (when the TED spread widens). These results seem counterfactual if one takes the interpretation that large unused commitments are a source of off-balance sheet liquidity risk. As Figure 4 shows, rather than hoarding government securities during the financial crisis, most banks were selling them; and rather than reducing their

---

[12]Cornett, McNutt, Strahan and Tehranian (2011) suggest a positive expected sign for loan commitments, but acknowledge the difficulty in establishing ex-ante the sign of this variable. As they argue, banks with greater unused commitments may be exposed to liquidity risk, but also experience greater increase in loan demand during the crisis.

[13]This result is somewhat in line with Ashcraft, McAndrews, and Skeie (2010), who find that small banks hold larger amounts of cash and excess reserves with the Federal Reserve than larger banks.

holdings of agency MBS, most banks decided to continue holding them. In contrast, the securities losses ratio (and more importantly, its interaction with the TED spread) consistently explains the behavior of each category of liquid assets. It significantly explains the increase in cash plus fed funds and the holdings of agency MBS. Securities losses and loan reserves also appear to be significant explanatory variables for the decline in government securities, in agreement with the behavior in Figure 4.

4.4 Liquidity Hoarding and Bank Size

As mentioned above, banks size seems to play a less significant role for liquidity hoarding. To further investigate the role of size, I conducted a regression analysis on each liquid asset category for large banks (assets above $1 billion) and small banks (assets below $1 billion), using the bank-size split in Cornett, McNutt, Strahan and Tehranian (2011). Results are shown in table 3. As before, the interactions between the TED spread and the variables that explain each liquid asset category are of particular interest. Core deposits and capital are more relevant for small banks than for large banks. The negative and significant coefficient on the interaction term of the TED spread and both core deposits and capital suggests that, during times of financial distress, core deposits and capital substitute for cash and fed funds for small banks. However, both funding sources seem to significantly explain the holdings of government securities and MBS during the financial crisis.

Table 3 also reveals that the complementarity between unused loan commitments, unrealized losses and loan loss reserves, is significantly important in explaining the cash hoarding of small banks during the financial crisis. However, this evidence seems weaker for large banks. To further examine the relationship between unused commitments and unrealized securities losses, Figure 5 plots the behavior of these two measures of liquidty risk for small and large banks. Unused commitments drop significantly for large banks, starting in September 2007, that is, immediately after the collapse of the interbank and the securitization markets (the unused commitment ratio falls from 16 percent in 2007:Q3 to 12 percent in 2009:Q2).[14] The decline in unused commitments

---

[14]This finding is consistent with Berrospide, Meisenzahl and Sullivan (2011), who report evidence of increased drawdowns of corporate credit lines starting in the fall of 2007, that is, earlier than previously documented.

continues during 2008, precisely when banks were hit by significant losses in their securities holdings. Securities losses for large banks rose to almost 2 percent after the collapse of Lehman and AIG in October 2008. Small banks faced a similar situation. Their unused commitments decreased from 9 percent to 7 percent during the financial crisis. Their securities losses increased from -1 percent (gain) to 1.6 percent between the first and third quarters of 2008.

4.4.1 Liquidity Hoarding of Very Large Banks

The results so far suggest that liquidity hoarding occurred across all banking institutions regardless of their size. Both large and small banks were highly exposed to a sudden drawdown in unused commitments, securities losses, and expected loan losses, and had the desire to hoard their cash reserves in anticipation of further write-downs. Moreover, funding risk from unused commitments was the driving force of liquidity hoarding mainly for large banks.

To further investigate the role of the different measures of liquidity risk during the financial crisis, I study the behavior of liquid assets, in particular the holdings of cash and fed funds, for very large banks (the largest 40 banks, with assets above $50 billion). As noted above, the valuation losses were significantly larger for the largest banks after mid-year 2007. These banks accounted for about 85 percent of the $52 billion of total securities losses in the banking sector at the height of the crisis.

Another source of liquidity risk faced by the largest banks during the financial crisis were the liquidity backstops and other forms of liquidity support to their conduits or Structured Investment Vehicles (SIVs) used in loan securitizations.[15] To account for this type of liquidity risk, I construct the variable *Conduit Exposure* (as a percent of total assets) by adding two items from Call Reports: (1) the maximum amount of credit exposure from credit enhancements to conduits (RCFDB806 and RCFDB807), and (2) the unused commitments to provide liquidity to conduits (RCFDB808

---

[15] As documented in Allen and Carletti (2008), and Brunnermeier (2009), when the market for asset-back commercial paper dried up, collateral values of even the safest (AAA-rated) tranches of securitized products dropped abruptly, forcing banks to either bring the underlying assets back to their balance sheets or to provide the committed support to their conduits. Their need for liquidity then rose dramatically.

and RCFDB809).[16] This measure of exposure to conduit structures exists only for the largest banks. I include this measure in the regression equation of the overall liquid asset ratio and the cash and fed funds to assets ratio for the largest banks.

Table 4 presents the estimation results. The coefficient of the interaction between the TED spread and the conduit exposure measure is positive and significant. This result suggests a key role of unused backup lines of liquidity that banks provided to their securitization conduits in explaining the cash hoarding of large banks during the financial crisis. Furthermore, *Conduit Exposure* seems to be another source of off-balance sheet risk which, together with unused loan commitments, exposed banks to liquidity risk stemming from sudden drawdowns from conduit structures and corporations, respectively. Table 4 also reveals that the risk posed by large undrawn loan and liqudity commitments acts in connection with unrealized losses in securities holdings to explain the hoarding of cash during times of financial distress. The interaction of the TED spread and each of these sources of liquidity risk is a key determinant of the increased holdings of liquid assets (mainly cash and fed funds) for the largest banks in the sample.

Figure 6 displays the behavior of the (quarterly) percent change of the two measures of off-balance sheet liquidity risk and the securities loss ratio for the largest banks. By plotting the change in unused loan and liquidity commitments, Figure 6 shows how off-balance sheet liquidity risks materialized during the financial crisis. The largest banks experienced increasing drawdowns of commited credit lines from corporations (negative changes) since the beginning of 2008. The drawdown of liquidity backup lines to conduits started earlier, as the securitization conduits experienced difficulties in rolling over ABCP in the fall of 2007, and increased dramatically in 2008. By year-end 2008, liquidity commitments to conduits fell by 25 percent.

Figure 6 also shows that the drawdown of unused commitments in 2008 occured at the time when the largest banks were severely hit by securities losses. The security loss ratio for these banks rose from zero to 5 percent in 2008 (an increase of approximately $25 billion in their balance sheets). A possible interpretation of this result is that corporations rushed to their banks to draw on their credit lines in anticipation of potential bank failures resulting from expected securities and

---

[16] These are obtained from schedule (RC-S), Servicing Securitization and Asset sale Activities.

loan losses, and further liquidity dry-ups.[17] This interpretation is also consistent with Ivashina and Scharfstein (2010), who argue that the drawdowns of commited revolving facilities from large corporations in syndicated markets (dominated by large banks) were a "run" on banks instigated by short-term creditors, counterparties, and borrowers who were concened about the liquidity and solvency of the banking sector.

4.5 Deposit Growth and Liquidity Hoarding

Previous work has raised concerns on the extent to which banks facing heightened liquidity risk are able to meet the increased borrowing demand from corporations shut out of the commercial paper market. As argued by Diamond and Rajan (2001) and empirically documented by Gatev and Strahan (2006) and Gatev, Schuermann, and Strahan (2009), commercial banks can cope with higher loan demand in the form of drawdowns of unused corporate credit lines as long as they are perceived as less risky and receive deposit inflows from institutional investors pulling their funds from securities markets (e.g. the commercial paper market).[18] Figure 7 depicts deposit flows of U.S. commercial banks between 2005 and 2010, and reveals a distinctive behavior of core and non-core deposits during two sub-periods of the financial crisis.

The growth rate of core deposits increased during the crisis, whereas the growth of non-core deposits contracted by almost fifty percent. Such behavior suggests a flight-to-quality effect in deposit flows. The upper panel of the figure shows that deposit growth, mainly non-core deposits, decreased remarkably over the second half of 2007. The sharp contraction in non-core deposits began immediately after the interbank markets—especially, the ABCP market—dried up. Furthermore, this sharp contraction continued through the first half of 2008, despite the significant decline in short-term interest rates that followed the reduction of the target federal funds rate from 5-1/4 percent in September 2007 to 2 percent by the spring of 2008. Deposit growth recovered months later, more notably during the fall of 2008. Intensifying turbulence in financial markets—

---

[17]This analysis is based on correlations only. A more rigorous causal analysis, which is beyond the purpose of this paper, may require the combined use of data on corporate credit lines, back-up liquidity lines to conduits, and bank balance sheet information.

[18]Core deposits include transaction deposits, savings deposits, and small time deposits (less than $100,000). Non-core deposits include large time deposits ($100,000 or more) and foreign deposits.

in particular after the failure of Lehman Brothers and AIG—caused significant outflows from money market mutual funds and contributed to the strong expansion of bank deposits. Favored by the increase in the deposit insurance limit from $100,000 to $250,000 and the implementation of the Temporary Liquidity Guarantee Program (TLGP) in October 2008, transaction deposits grew considerably (about one-fifth) in 2008.

The lower panel of Figure 7 shows the growth rate of core and non-core deposits by liquidity-hoarding banks and their non-hoarding counterparts. Before the crisis, the growth rates of both core and non-core deposits were lower for liquidity hoarders (red line). This situation reverses during the first year of the financial crisis for core deposits. Deposits increased significantly as liquidity fled other markets and is mainly explained by flows to liquidity-hoarding banks. Non-hoarding banks seemed to attract core deposits at a slower pace. However, as the crisis deepened during the fall of 2008, liquidity hoarders saw a sharp contraction in their core deposits, whereas non-hoarding banks continued to receive such deposits. One interpretation for such different behavior between liquidity hoarders and non-hoarders is that banks highly exposed to credit and securities losses managed to attract deposits at the beginning of the crisis (during the first year) by raising their deposit rates. This interpretation is consistent with Acharya and Mora (2011), who find that banks hit by a funding squeeze attempted to attract deposits by raising their deposit rates. At the height of the crisis, however, depositors lost confidence and these banks were perceived as more risky institutions as some of their losses started to materialize. Less exposed banks (non-hoarders of liquidity) faced lower risks and managed to continue receiving core deposits. In contrast to the surge in core deposits, non-core deposits decreased sharply for both hoarders and non-hoarders at about the same pace.

Taken together, these findings suggest a flight-to-quality effect from non-core to core deposits. Non-core deposits flew out of both types of banks at similar rates, and returned in the form of core deposits to liquidity hoarders at first, and to non-hoarders at the peak of the crisis. More importantly, this flight-to-quality seems to have occurred within the banking sector, and, therefore, complements the flight-to-quality effect documented by Gatev and Strahan (2006).

To summarize, during the recent financial turmoil many banking institutions had enormous difficulties accessing short-term debt markets. In those circumstances, it is also likely that within the banking sector—where institutions are more harshly competing for liquid funds—banks perceived as a safe haven for deposits (with large holdings of liquid assets) benefited more than less liquid banks and were able to attract inflows in the form of core deposits by raising their rates. As Pennacchi (2006) suggests, investors regard banks as a "safe haven" only when they can be confident that their deposits are insured or backed by a government guarantee. My findings suggest that core (insured) deposits added liquidity to banks that wanted to hoard their liquid funds.

4.6 Determinants of the Decision to Hoard Liquid Assets

Since I can identify the quarter when a bank switches from not hoarding to hoarding liquidity, I investigate the determinants of the decision to hoard liquid assets. This is done using a Cox-Proportional Hazard Model, which better captures the dynamics in the decision to start hoarding liquidity.[19] In this framework, the dependent variable is a binary variable intended to measure the probability that a bank decides to start hoarding liquid assets at time t, conditional on the fact that it did not hoard liquidity as of $t-1$.

The bank's decision to start hoarding liquid assets is modeled as a function of its own characteristics, such as size, capitalization, and availability of deposits. These variables are measured at the beginning of each period (previous quarter). I also include quarter fixed effects to capture time-varying characteristics affecting all banks equally. As before, the main variables of interest are the measures of risk: unused commitments, loan loss reserves as a proxy for future losses in bank loan portfolios, and exposure to losses in securities portfolios.

Table 5 presents the estimation results using the same specifications but for two models. In model 1, the dummy variable identifying a bank that starts hoarding liquidity is based on the

---

[19]Unlike a probit model used to estimate the probability that a bank is a liquidity hoarder (the dummy variable describing hoarding banks is time-invariant), in the proportional hazard model the dependent variable varies over time as the deterioration in financial markets continues to cause more and more banks to accumulate liquid assets. In unreported probit regressions, I also find that securities losses and loan reserves have significant explanatory power for the probability of liquidity hoarding.

share of cash and fed funds (including reverse repos) to total assets. In model 2 this variable is measured based on the overall ratio of liquid assets to total assets. Both bank size and bank capital are significant and negatively correlated with the decision to start hoarding liquid assets, which suggests that smaller and less capitalized banks become liquidity hoarders sooner than large and more capitalized banks. Even after controlling for those time-varying bank-specific characteristics, I find strong and significant coefficients on my proposed proxies for on balance sheet risks (i.e. securities losses and loan loss reserves) in model 1, in which liquidity hoarding banks are identified by increased cash and fed fund hondings. The evidence for securities losses as a measure of liqudity risk is weak in model 2, in which liqudity hoarding banks are identified by an increase in the overall liquid asset ratio. A potential explanation for this result is that liquid assets that exclude securities, that is, only excess reserves in the form of cash, fed funds and reverse repos, are used by banks for the purpose of liquidity hoarding. As shown in Figure 4, during the financial crisis banks increased their holdings of agency MBS but also had to sell government securties to cope with increasing funding pressures.

The estimates are consistent with my hypothesis that banks hoard cash in response to future expected losses and write-downs. Moreover, unlike off-balance sheet liquidity risk stemming from potential drawdowns of committed loans, my proposed measures of on-balance sheet liquidity risks seem to explain more accurately the decision to hoard liquid assets. The coefficient on unused commitments is significant but negative.

4.7 Effect of Liquidity Hoarding on Bank Lending

After establishing the result that banks hoard liquidity in response to increased risks in their asset portfolios, particularly during times of financial stress in short-term funding markets (when the TED spread widens), I next test the effects of liquidity hoarding on bank loan growth. I use the following regression specification for the quarterly growth rate of bank loans:

$$\Delta\%Loan_{i,t} = \sum_{s=1}^{3} \alpha_s \Delta\%Loan_{i,t-s} + \sum_{s=1}^{3} \gamma_s \Delta\%GDP_{i,t-s} + \lambda Liquid + \sum_{s=1}^{3} \beta_s \Delta TED_{t-s} * Liquid$$
$$+ \sum_{s=1}^{3} \chi_s CHG_{i,t-s} + \epsilon_{i,t}$$

(1)

In this specification, economic growth $\Delta\%GDP$ is included to control for changes in loan demand, and the fraction of net charge-offs to total assets CHG is a measure of credit quality.[20] $Liquid$ is a dummy variable that takes the value of 1 for banks identified as liquidity hoarders and 0 otherwise. As expected, when a bank hoards liquidity it has fewer funds available to lend, and therefore, the coefficient on $Liquid$ should be negative, ($\lambda < 0$). The effect of changes in the TED spread interacted with $Liquid$ is also of particular interest. If the TED spread is an accurate description of the severe stress in interbank and other short-term funding markets, and it causes more liquidity hoarding through the effects on expected losses in banks' asset portfolios, then one would expect a negative impact on lending for banks that hoard liquidity ($\beta_s < 0$).

The decision to hoard liquid assets is, of course, endogenous. For example, a bank may decide to hoard liquid assets in response to a lack of lending opportunities. Thus, it is possible that the causality runs from less lending to increased holdings of liquid assets. To address endogeneity concerns, and given that I already model the determinants of the decision to hoard liquid assets (using both a probit model and a proportional hazard model), I also run regression (1) replacing the dummy variable $Liquid$ with the predicted values of the decision to hoard liquidity (from a probit model).[21]

---

[20] As in Cornet, Mc Nutt, Strahan, and Tehranian (2011), in (unreported) alternative specifications, I find that the sources of liquidity risk (including securities losses) that explain increased holdings of liquid assets also explain the contraction in the loan growth rate during the crisis. I prefer specification (1) as it estimates a loan supply relationship and controls for credit quality and loan demand factors.

[21] Another robustness check I consider to deal with endogeneity is a methodology proposed by Faulkender and Peterson (2011). In this case, regression (1) includes not only the predicted value for the decision to hoard liquidity but also a residual (unexplained) component of liquidity hoarding given by the difference between the actual dummy $Liquid$ and its predicted value. By including these two components, the regression specification controls for the likelihood of being a liquidity hoarder and, conditional on the decision to hoard liquidity, the residual component identifies the effect of liquidity hoarding on loan growth. I obtained similar results using this method.

The estimation results using OLS regressions are reported in Table 6. The table shows four different specifications: the first two columns use the dummy variable *Liquid* to identify liquidity-hoarding banks and the last two use its predicted value. Models 1 and 3 include the liquidity hoarding variable only, whereas models 2 and 4 add the interaction term between the changes in the TED spread and the liquidity hoarding variable. All variables enter the regressions with the expected sign and are statistically significant. For example, the positive and significant coefficient on economic growth suggests that loan growth increases with higher loan demand. The negative and significant coefficient on the charge-off rate suggests that deterioration in borrower quality reduces bank loan growth. The negative coefficients on the liquidity hoarding dummy in model 1 suggest that, on average, liquidity-hoarding banks reduce their quarterly loan growth about 1.3 percent more than non-hoarding banks. More importantly, the regression results in model 2 provide evidence that, compared to non-hoarding banks, an increase in the TED spread reduces significantly the loan growth of liquidity-hoarding banks.

In short, consistent with previous work documenting the substantial real and financial effects of disruptions in interbank markets, estimates using model 2 indicate that a 10-basis-point increase in the change of the TED spread reduces the annualized growth of bank loans of liquidity hoarders by 1.26 percentage points. Between 2007:Q2 and 2008:Q4 the change in the TED spread increased by about 90 basis points, while the annualized growth rate of bank loans fell 12 percentage points during the same period. My estimates indicate that liquidity hoarding banks reduced their loan growth by 3.4 percentage points. Taking into account that such contraction in bank lending results from the hoarding of liquidity in response to increased risks during financial distress (i.e. due to precautionary reasons), this result suggests an important economic effect: more than one fourth of the reduction in bank lending during the crisis is explained by precautionary liquidity hoarding.

5 Conclusion

This paper studies the main determinants of bank liquidity hoarding during the recent financial crisis. Consistent with theoretical explanations for the precautionary motive of liquidity hoarding, the empirical results show that banks choose to build up liquidity in anticipation of future expected losses from securities write-downs.

Compared with previously suggested proxies for banks' liquidity risk—such as the proportion of unused loan commitments to their lending capacity—exposure to securities losses in their investment portfolio represents a more accurate measure of liquidity risk associated with the run in repo markets during the financial crisis. This measure of liquidity risk is consistent with the theory of liquidity hoarding reviewed in the paper and provides supporting evidence for the precautionary motive. I also find evidence that loan loss reserves are another key factor contributing to the increased holdings of liquid assets, especially for small banks. Although not a substitute for cash, and thus less related to liquidity risk, the forward-looking component of loan loss reserves seems to reflect banks' asset reallocation from loans (which have become riskier due to the reduced creditworthiness of their borrowers) to safe and liquid securities.

The paper also documents an important flight-to-quality effect in deposit flows. Consistent with the view that deposits represent a stable source of funds for bank operations, I find evidence of inflows of core deposits during the financial crisis to banks that chose to hoard liquidity. Non-core deposits flew from both liquidity-hoarding and non-hoarding banks, moving into hoarding banks in the form of core deposits. Finally, the paper also finds evidence consistent with previous work documenting the substantial real and financial effects of disruptions in interbank markets. I find that for liquidity-hoarding banks, more than one-fourth of the lending contraction is due to the precautionary motive.

References

[1] Acharya, Viral V., D. Gromb, and T. Yorulmazer, 2009, Imperfect Competition in the Interbank Market for Liquidity as a Rationale for Central Banking, Working Paper, New York University Stern School of Business.

[2] Acharya, Viral V. and Ouarda Merrouche, 2010, Precautionary Hoarding of Liquidity and Interbank Markets: Evidence from Subprime Crisis, Working paper, New York University Stern School of Business.

[3] Acharya, Viral V. and N. Mora, 2011, Are Banks Passive Liquidity Backstops? Deposit Rates and Flows during the 2007-2009 Crisis, Working paper, New York University Stern School of Business.

[4] Acharya, Viral V. and D. Skeie, 2011, A Model of Liquidity Hoarding and Term Premia in Interbank Markets, Working paper, Federal Reserve Bank of New York, Staff Report No 498.

[5] Allen, Franklin and Carletti Elena, 2008, The Role of Liquidity in Financial Crises, Jackson Hole Conference Proceedings, Federal Reserve Bank of Kansas City, 379-412.

[6] Allen, Franklin and Douglas Gale, 2004, Financial Fragility, Liquidity, and Asset Prices, *Journal of the European Economic Association* vol. 3, pp. 533-546.

[7] Allen, Franklin and Douglas Gale, 2000, Financial Contagion, *Journal of Political Economy* vol. 108(1), pp. 1-33.

[8] Ashcraft, Adam, James Mc Andrews, and David Skeie, 2010, Precautionary Reserves and the Interbank Market, *Journal of Money, Credit and Banking*, forthcoming.

[9] Berger, A. N. and C. H. S. Bouwman, 2009, Bank Liquidity Creation, *Review of Financial Studies* vol. 22, pp. 3779-3837.

[10] Berrospide, Jose, Ralf Meisenzahl, and Briana Sullivan, 2012, Credit Line Use and Availability in the Financial Crisis: The Importance of Hedging, Finance and Economics Discussion Series, 2012-27. Board of Governors of the Federal Reserve System.

[11] Brunnermeir, Markus, 2009, Deciphering the liquidity and credit crunch 2007-2008, *Journal of Economic Perspectives* vol. 23, pp. 77-100.

[12] Caballero, Ricardo J. and Alp Simsek, 2009, Complexity and Financial Panics, NBER Working Paper No. 14997.

[13] Caballero, Ricardo J. and A. Krishnamurthy, 2008, Collective Risk Management in a Flight-to-Quality Episode, *Journal of Finance*, vol. 63, pp. 2195-2230.

[14] Cornett, Marcia, Jamie J. McNutt, Philip Strahan, and Hassan Tehranian, 2011, Liquidity Risk Management and Credit Supply in the Financial Crisis, *Journal of Financial Economics* vol. 101(2), pp. 297-312.

[15] Covitz, Daniel, Nellie Liang, and Gustavo Suarez, 2012, The evolution of a Financial Crisis: Collapse of the Asset-Backed Commercial Paper Market, *Journal of Finance*, forthcoming.

[16] De Haan, Leo, and Jan W. van den End, 2011, Banks responses to funding liquidity shocks: Lending adjustment, liquidity hoarding, and fire sales, De Nederlandsche Bank, Working Paper.

[17] Diamond, Douglas, and Raghuram Rajan, 2009, Fear of Fire Sales, Illiquidity Seeking and the Credit Freeze, *Quarterly Journal of Economics*, forthcoming.

[18] Faulkender, Michael and Mitchell Peterson, 2011, Investment and Capital Constraints: Repatriations Under the American Jobs Creation Act, Manuscript, Northwestern University.

[19] Gale, Douglas, and Tanju Yorulmazer, 2012, Liquidity Hoarding, *Theoretical Economics*, forthcoming.

[20] Gatev, Evan, Til Schuermann, and Philip Strahan, 2009, Managing Bank Liquidity Risk: How Deposit-Loan Synergies Vary with Market Conditions, *Review of Financial Studies* vol. 22(3), pp. 995-1020.

[21] Gatev, Evan and Philip Strahan, 2006, Banks' Advantage in Hedging Liquidity Risk: Theory and Evidence from the Commercial Paper Market, *Journal of Finance* vol. 61, pp. 867-92.

[22] Gorton, Gary, 2010, Information, Liquidity, and the (Ongoing) Panic of 2007, *American Economic Review, Papers and Proceedings* vol. 99(2), pp. 567-572.

[23] Hancock Diana and Wayne Passmore, 2011, QE2 and the Federal Reserves Effects on Mortgage Markets, Board of Governors of the Federal Reserve System, Working Paper.

[24] Heider, Florian, Marie Hoerova, and Cornelia Holthausen, 2008, Liquidity Hoarding and Interbank Market Spreads: The Role of Counterparty Risk, WP, European Central Bank.

[25] Ivashina, Victoria, and David S. Scharfstein, 2010, Bank Lending During the Financial Crisis of 2008, *Journal of Financial Economics* vol. 97(3), pp. 319-338.

[26] Martin Antoine, James McAndrews and David Skeie, 2011, A Note on Bank Lending in Times of Large Bank Reserves, Federal Reserve Bank of New York Staff Report No. 497.

[27] Pennacchi, George, 2006, Deposit Insurance, bank regulation, and financial system risks, *Journal of Monetary Economics* vol. 53, pp. 1-30.

[28] Ramos Alberto, 1996, Deposit Insurance, Bank Capital Structures and the Demand for Liquidity, Working Paper Series (WP-96-8), Federal Reserve Bank of Chicago.

[29] Strahan, Philip, 2008, Liquidity Production in 21st Century Banking, NBER WP No. 13798.

[30] Wolman, Alexander and H. Ennis, 2011, Large Excess Reserves in the U.S.: A View from the Cross-Section of Banks, Federal Reserve Bank of Richmond, Manuscript.

[31] Zawadowski, Adam, 2011, Interwoven Lending, Uncertainty and Liquidity Hoarding, Boston University, Working Paper.

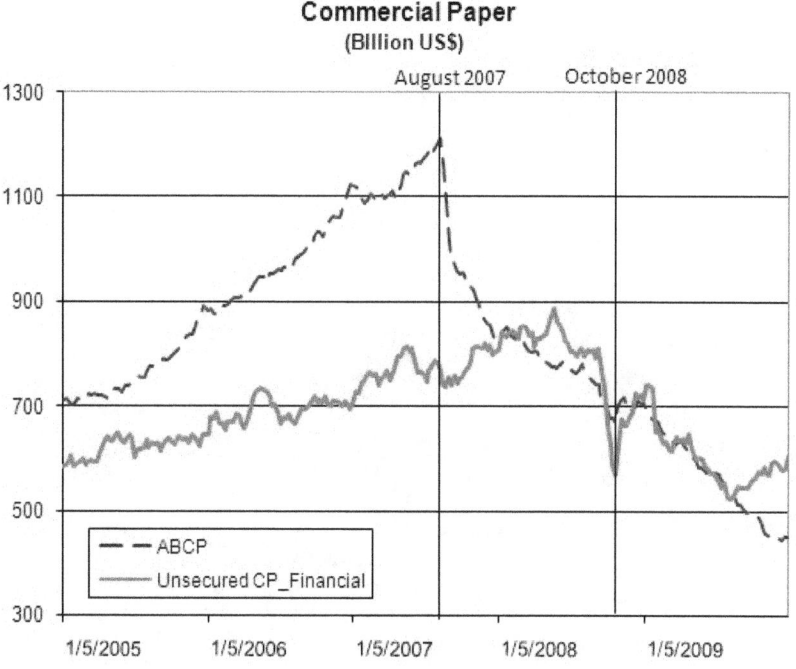

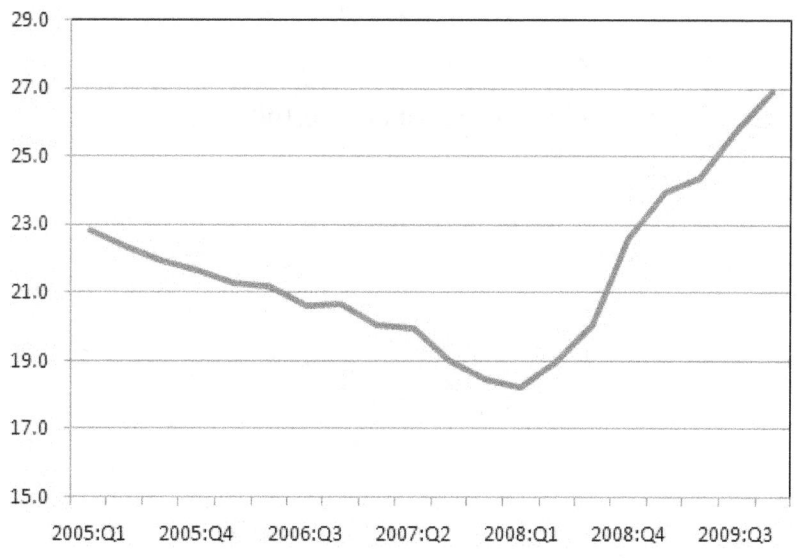

1/ Liquid Assets include cash, balances from depository institutions and investment securities.

Figure 1: Disruption in Short-term Funding Markets and Bank Liquidity Hoarding

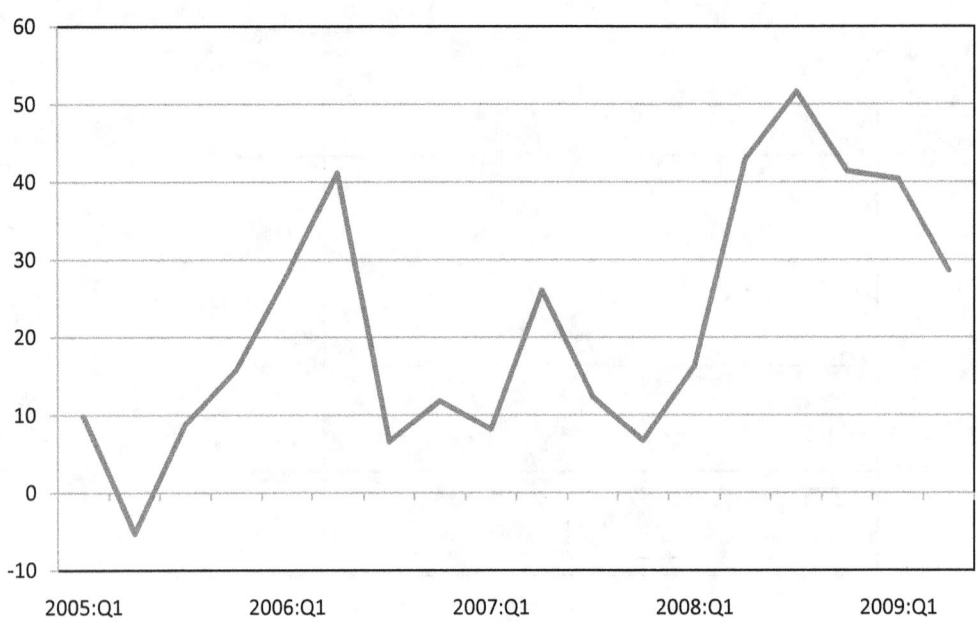

Figure 2: Bank Securities Losses (Billion US$)

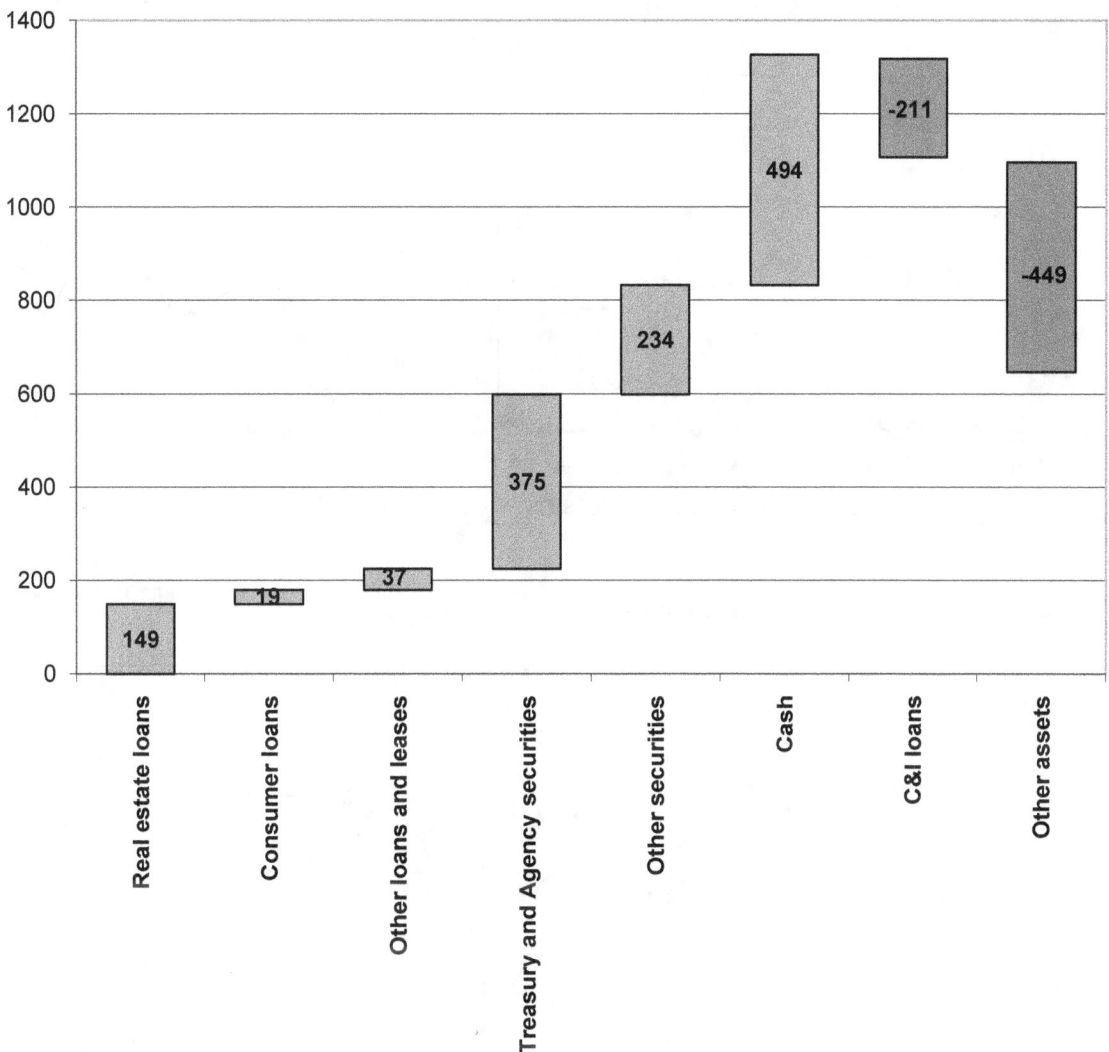

Source: Federal Deposit Insurance Corporation (FDIC).

Figure 3: Changes in Commercial Bank Assets: 2008 and 2009 (Billion US$)

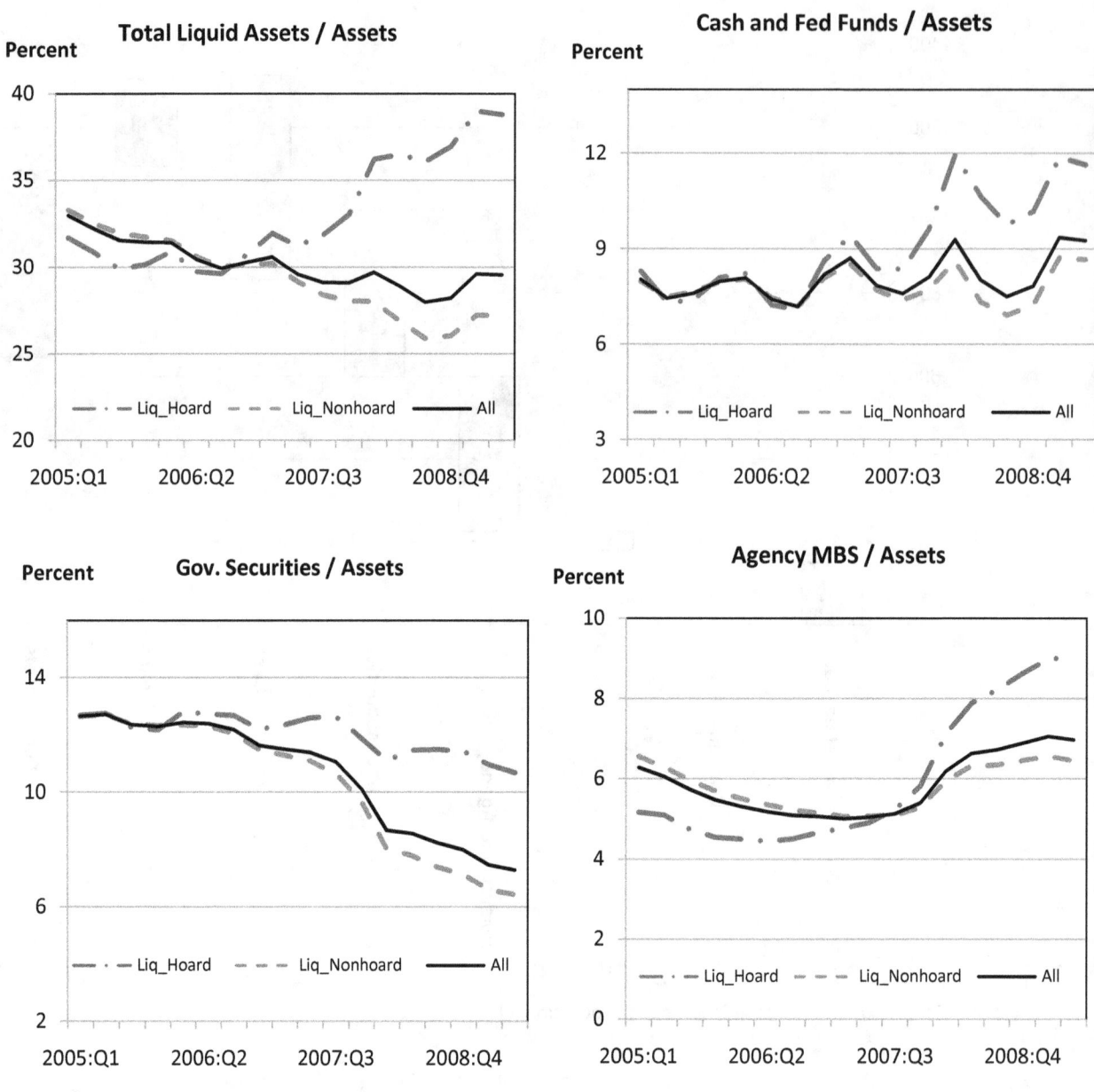

Figure 4: Liquidity Hoarding, U.S. Commercial Banks: 2005-2009

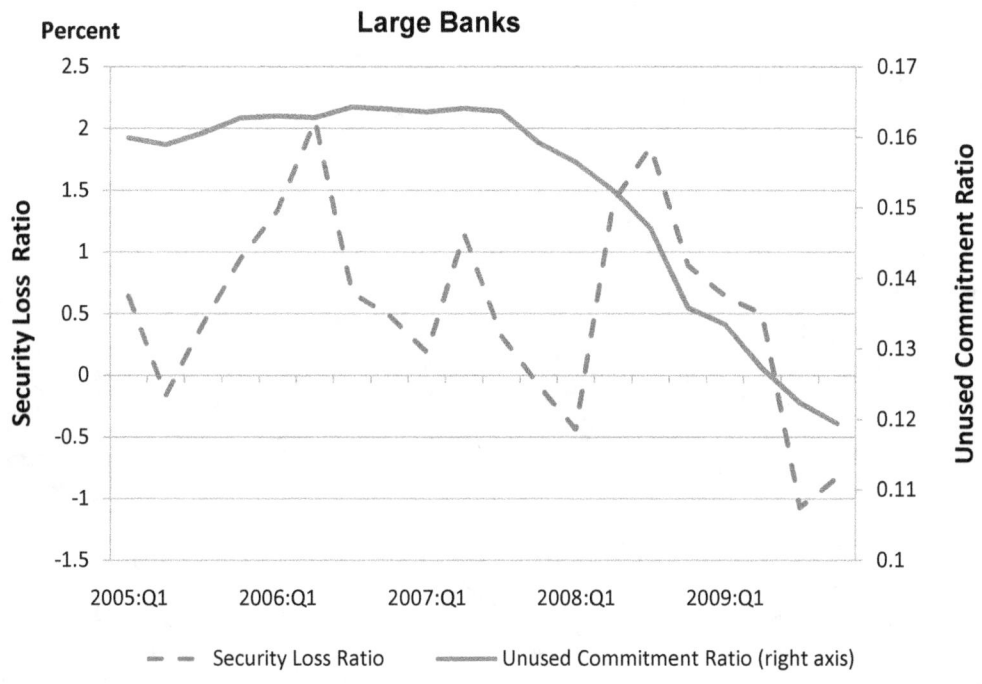

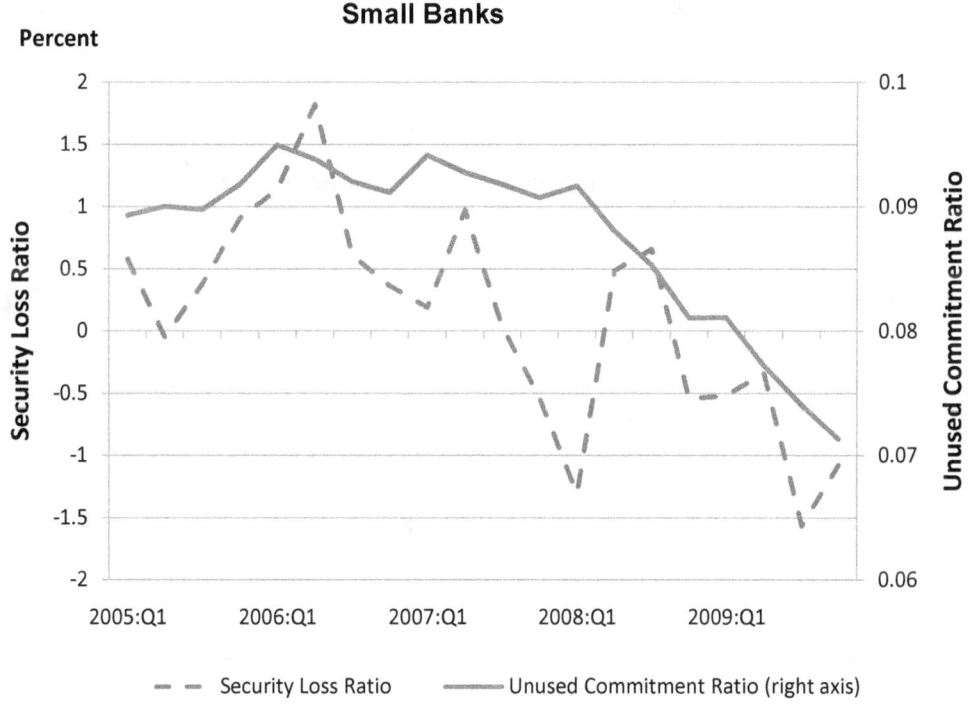

Figure 5: Unused Commitments and Securities Losses by Bank Size

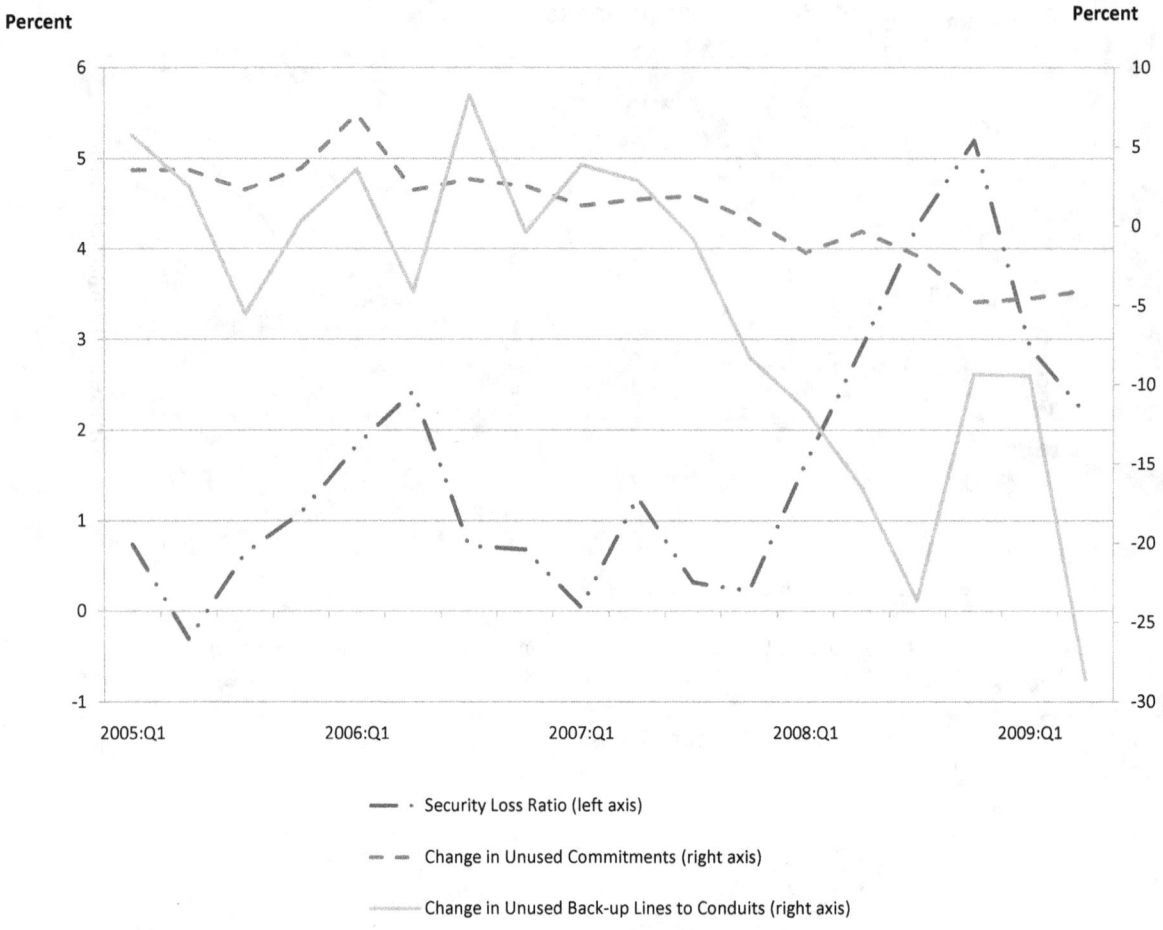

Figure 6: Liquidity Hoarding Incentives, Very Large Commercial Banks (Assets ≥ $50 Billion)

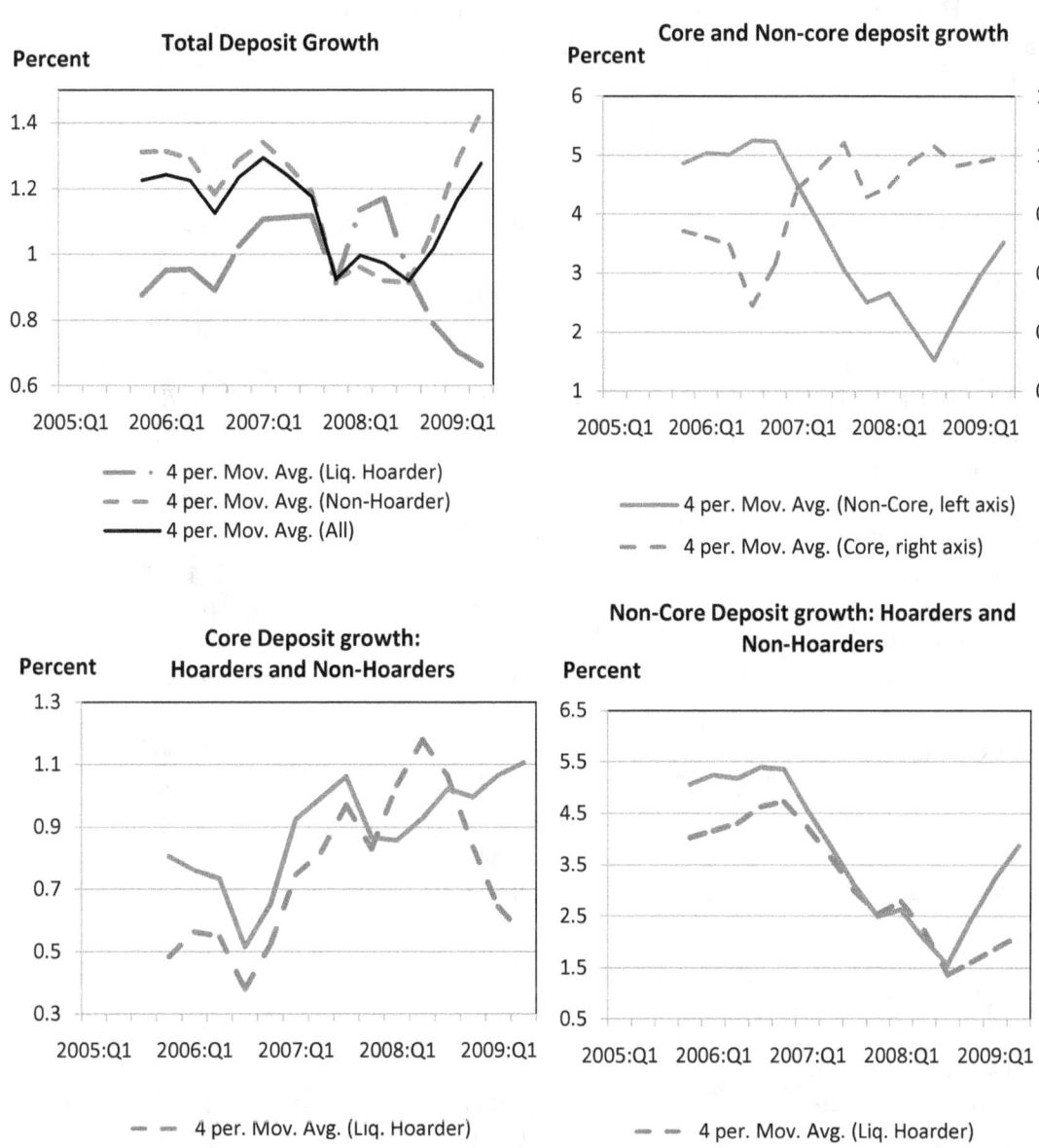

Figure 7: Deposit Growth (Quarterly growth rates, 4-period moving average)

Table 1: Bank Characteristics by Liquidity Hoarding Groups (Sample means)

Variable	Before Crisis	Crisis
Panel A: Liquidity Non-Hoarder		
Assets ($ Million)	1420.79	1650.07
Tier1 Capital ratio	0.165	0.156
Loan Growth (% quarter)	2.236	1.807
Liquid Asset / Assets	0.311	0.272
Illiq. Asset / Assets	0.707	0.747
Unused Commit. ratio	0.099	0.093
Security Loss ratio	0.669	-0.168
Loan Reserve / Loans	1.340	1.375
Total Deposit growth	1.214	1.172
Core Deposit growth	0.760	1.013
Trans. Deposit growth	0.437	1.381
Net Charge-offs / Assets	0.113	0.358
Panel B: Liquidity Hoarder		
Assets ($ Million)	1840.67	2444.57
Tier1 Capital ratio	0.169	0.171
Loan Growth (% quarter)	1.22	-0.078
Liquid Asset / Assets	0.307	0.360
Illiq. Asset / Assets	0.699	0.679
Unused Commit. ratio	0.089	0.080
Security Loss ratio	0.835	-0.229
Loan Reserve / Loans	1.436	1.578
Total Deposit growth	0.843	0.905
Core Deposit growth	0.468	0.857
Trans. Deposit growth	0.151	1.556
Net Charge-offs / Assets	0.169	0.379
Panel C: All Banks		
Assets ($ Million)	1504.16	1812.10
Tier1 Capital ratio	0.166	0.159
Loan growth (% quarter)	2.035	1.423
Liquid Asset / Assets	0.310	0.291
Illiq. Asset / Assets	0.706	0.733
Unused Commit. ratio	0.097	0.091
Security Loss ratio	0.702	-0.180
Loan Reserve / Loans	1.359	1.417
Total Deposit growth	1.141	1.118
Core Deposit growth	0.702	0.981
Trans. Deposit growth	0.380	1.417
Net Charge-offs / Assets	0.124	0.363

Table 2: Fixed Effect Regressions of Various Liquid Assets

	Model 1		Model 2			
	$\Delta Liq.Asset/$ $Assets_{t-1}$ (1)	$\Delta(Cash+FF)/$ $Assets_{t-1}$ (2)	$\Delta Liq.Asset/$ $Assets_{t-1}$ (3)	$\Delta(Cash+FF)/$ $Assets_{t-1}$ (4)	$\Delta Gov.Sec./$ $Assets_{t-1}$ (5)	$\Delta MBSAg/$ $Assets_{t-1}$ (6)
$Log\ Asset_{t-1}$	-0.032***	-0.027***	-0.033***	-0.028***	-0.001*	-0.003***
	(0.002)	(0.001)	(0.002)	(0.002)	(0.001)	(0.000)
$Log\ Asset_{t-1}*TED$	-0.115***	-0.168***	-0.113***	-0.163***	-0.004	0.066***
	(0.019)	(0.017)	(0.019)	(0.017)	(0.009)	(0.006)
$Tier1\ Cap\ rat_{t-1}$	-0.020***	0.013*	-0.024***	0.013*	-0.013***	-0.025***
	(0.007)	(0.007)	(0.007)	(0.008)	(0.004)	(0.002)
$Tier1\ Cap\ rat_{t-1}*TED$	-0.362	-2.678***	-0.303	-2.642***	1.264***	0.681***
	(0.349)	(0.372)	(0.349)	(0.386)	(0.235)	(0.130)
$Core\ Dep/Asset_{t-1}$	-0.019***	-0.026***	-0.020***	-0.029***	0.005***	0.001
	(0.004)	(0.003)	(0.004)	(0.003)	(0.002)	(0.001)
$Core\ Dep/Asset_{t-1}*TED$	-0.262	-1.114***	-0.259	-1.107***	0.509***	0.181**
	(0.221)	(0.211)	(0.224)	(0.210)	(0.110)	(0.076)
$Illiq\ Asset/Asset_{t-1}$	0.226***	0.247***	0.226***	0.250***	0.004*	-0.030***
	(0.004)	(0.004)	(0.004)	(0.004)	(0.002)	(0.001)
$Illiq\ Asset/Asset_{t-1}*TED$	0.042	-0.936***	0.251	-0.744***	1.160***	0.012
	(0.211)	(0.214)	(0.212)	(0.215)	(0.131)	(0.069)
$Unused\ Commit\ rat_{t-1}$	-0.144***	-0.132***	-0.144***	-0.126***	-0.029***	0.004**
	(0.007)	(0.006)	(0.007)	(0.006)	(0.003)	(0.002)
$Unused\ Commit\ rat_{t-1}*TED$	2.414***	2.203***	2.331***	1.984***	1.353***	-0.823***
	(0.457)	(0.432)	(0.460)	(0.436)	(0.224)	(0.139)
$Sec\ Loss\ rat_{t-1}$			-0.002	-0.005	0.009***	0.0001
			(0.005)	(0.005)	(0.002)	(0.001)
$Sec\ Loss\ rat_{t-1}*TED$			0.688*	0.994**	-0.573***	0.346***
			(0.400)	(0.403)	(0.186)	(0.113)
$Loan\ Reserve/Loan_{t-1}$			-0.001	0.0004	0.0004	-0.001***
			(0.001)	(0.001)	(0.0003)	(0.0002)
$Loan\ Reserve/Loan_{t-1}*TED$			0.079**	0.119***	-0.033*	-0.007
			(0.035)	(0.035)	(0.019)	(0.011)
Intercept	0.248***	0.179***	0.268***	0.189***	0.010	0.058***
	(0.019)	(0.019)	(0.020)	(0.020)	(0.008)	(0.005)
Firm Dummies	Yes	Yes	Yes	Yes	Yes	Yes
Quart. Dummies	Yes	Yes	Yes	Yes	Yes	Yes
R^2	0.220	0.213	0.221	0.216	0.106	0.173
Observ.	109494	109494	108700	108700	108700	108700

Standard errors are in parentheses. *, **, *** denotes significance at 10%, 5% and 1% levels.

Table 3: Fixed Effect Regressions of Various Liquid Assets by Bank Size

	Large Banks			Small Banks		
	$\Delta(Cash+FF)/$ $Assets_{t-1}$ (1)	$\Delta Gov.Sec./$ $Assets_{t-1}$ (2)	$\Delta MBSAg/$ $Assets_{t-1}$ (3)	$\Delta(Cash+FF)/$ $Assets_{t-1}$ (4)	$\Delta Gov.Sec./$ $Assets_{t-1}$ (5)	$\Delta MBSAg/$ $Assets_{t-1}$ (6)
$Log\ Asset_{t-1}$	-0.012***	-0.003	-0.003*	-0.033***	-0.001**	-0.003***
	(0.004)	(0.002)	(0.002)	(0.001)	(0.001)	(0.0004)
$Log\ Asset_{t-1}*TED$	0.126**	0.079***	-0.011	-0.284***	-0.025*	0.071***
	(0.052)	(0.025)	(0.027)	(0.024)	(0.013)	(0.008)
$Tier1\ Cap\ rat_{t-1}$	-0.057*	-0.013	-0.015	0.012	-0.014***	-0.025***
	(0.032)	(0.013)	(0.012)	(0.008)	(0.004)	(0.003)
$Tier1\ Cap\ rat_{t-1}*TED$	-3.093	1.479*	-0.724	-2.911***	1.233***	0.724***
	(2.094)	(0.778)	(0.587)	(0.393)	(0.242)	(0.133)
$Core\ Dep/Asset_{t-1}$	0.008	-0.002	0.001	-0.038***	0.005***	0.001
	(0.009)	(0.004)	(0.004)	(0.004)	(0.002)	(0.001)
$Core\ Dep/Asset_{t-1}*TED$	-0.749	0.294	-0.153	-1.135***	0.559***	0.194**
	(0.551)	(0.248)	(0.276)	(0.229)	(0.122)	(0.080)
$Illiq\ Asset/Asset_{t-1}$	0.167***	0.013*	-0.031***	0.254***	0.003	-0.030***
	(0.014)	(0.008)	(0.006)	(0.004)	(0.002)	(0.001)
$Illiq\ Asset/Asset_{t-1}*TED$	0.942	1.220***	-0.152	-0.588***	1.218***	-0.012
	(0.738)	(0.423)	(0.286)	(0.226)	(0.139)	(0.073)
$Unused\ Commit\ rat_{t-1}$	-0.057***	-0.007	0.029***	-0.132***	-0.031***	0.003
	(0.018)	(0.012)	(0.010)	(0.007)	(0.003)	(0.002)
$Unused\ Commit\ rat_{t-1}*TED$	0.575	0.787	-1.251**	1.974***	1.361***	-0.736***
	(0.975)	(0.605)	(0.488)	(0.477)	(0.243)	(0.146)
$Sec\ Loss\ rat_{t-1}$	0.006	0.009	-0.008	-0.006	0.009***	0.0003
	(0.022)	(0.011)	(0.008)	(0.005)	(0.002)	(0.001)
$Sec\ Loss\ rat_{t-1}*TED$	0.709	-0.136	1.432*	0.916**	-0.593***	0.304***
	(2.028)	(0.816)	(0.743)	(0.411)	(0.191)	(0.114)
$Loan\ Reserve/Loan_{t-1}$	-0.001	-0.001	-0.001**	0.001	0.0004	-0.001***
	(0.002)	(0.001)	(0.001)	(0.001)	(0.0003)	(0.0002)
$Loan\ Reserve/Loan_{t-1}*TED$	0.018	0.021	0.063	0.092**	-0.038*	-0.009
	(0.120)	(0.074)	(0.050)	(0.036)	(0.020)	(0.012)
Intercept	0.062	0.025	0.067***	0.252***	0.015	0.058***
	(0.063)	(0.034)	(0.026)	(0.018)	(0.009)	(0.005)
Firm Dummies	Yes	Yes	Yes	Yes	Yes	Yes
Quart. Dummies	Yes	Yes	Yes	Yes	Yes	Yes
R^2	0.175	0.156	0.189	0.224	0.107	0.175
Observ.	8170	8170	8170	100530	100530	100530

Standard errors are in parentheses. *, **, *** denotes significance at 10%, 5% and 1% levels.

Table 4: Liquidity Hoarding of Very Large Banks

	$\Delta Liq.Asset/Assets_{t-1}$ (1)	$\Delta (Cash+FF)/Assets_{t-1}$ (2)
$Log\ Asset_{t-1}$	-0.025**	-0.024*
	(0.012)	(0.014)
$Log\ Asset_{t-1}*TED$	-0.475	-0.390
	(0.292)	(0.331)
$Tier1\ Cap\ rat_{t-1}$	0.186	0.120
	(0.275)	(0.278)
$Tier1\ Cap\ rat_{t-1}*TED$	-13.449	-7.623
	(17.197)	(16.781)
$Core\ Dep/Asset_{t-1}$	-0.086**	-0.060
	(0.040)	(0.043)
$Core\ Dep/Asset_{t-1}*TED$	2.864	3.771
	(2.735)	(3.340)
$Illiq\ Asset/Asset_{t-1}$	0.267***	0.234***
	(0.043)	(0.049)
$Illiq\ Asset/Asset_{t-1}*TED$	-3.921	-4.322
	(2.718)	(3.155)
$Unused\ Commit\ rat_{t-1}$	0.326**	0.328**
	(0.156)	(0.161)
$Unused\ Commit\ rat_{t-1}*TED$	13.199**	8.938
	(6.106)	(6.945)
$Sec\ Loss\ rat_{t-1}$	-0.051	-0.164
	(0.129)	(0.133)
$Sec\ Loss\ rat_{t-1}*TED$	17.196**	18.100**
	(7.250)	(7.660)
$Loan\ Reserve/Loan_{t-1}$	0.004	0.002
	(0.006)	(0.006)
$Loan\ Reserve/Loan_{t-1}*TED$	-0.142	-0.133
	(0.455)	(0.477)
$Conduit\ Expo/Asset_{t-1}$	-0.035	-0.054
	(0.102)	(0.101)
$Conduit\ Expo/Asset_{t-1}*TED$	23.381***	20.310**
	(7.076)	(7.865)
Intercept	0.223	0.226
	(0.250)	(0.279)
Firm Dummies	Yes	Yes
Quart. Dummies	Yes	Yes
R^2	0.387	0.332
Observ.	477	477

Standard errors are in parentheses. *, **, *** denotes significance at 10%, 5% and 1% levels.

Table 5: Cox Proportional Hazard Model: Determinants of the decision to be Liquidity Hoarder

	Model 1 Using $(Cash + FedFunds)/Assets$ (1)	Model 2 Using $Liq.Assets/Assets$ (2)
$Unused\ Commit\ rat_{t-1}$	-1.563**	-2.859**
	(0.695)	(0.641)
$Log\ Asset_{t-1}$	-0.322***	-0.109***
	(0.037)	(0.029)
$Tier1\ Cap\ rat_{t-1}$	-2.122***	-3.385***
	(0.408)	(0.440)
$Sec\ Loss\ rat_{t-1}$	1.796***	0.393
	(0.473)	(0.512)
$Loan\ Reserve/Loan_{t-1}$	0.193***	0.264***
	(0.036)	(0.032)
$Core\ Dep/Asset_{t-1}$	1.183***	0.881***
	(0.330)	(0.304)
$Illiq\ Asset/Asset_{t-1}$	-2.963***	-2.314***
	(0.248)	(0.253)
Observ.	55946	54725
Quart. Dummies	Yes	Yes

Standard errors are in parentheses. *, **, *** denotes significance at 10%, 5% and 1% levels.

Table 6: Effect of Liquidity Hoarding on Bank Loan Growth

	Model 1 Liquid Dummy (1)	Model 2 Liquid Dummy (2)	Model 3 Liquid hat (3)	Model 4 Liquid hat (4)
Sum of lagged loan growth	0.295***	0.294***	0.303***	0.303***
Sum of lagged GDP growth	0.408***	0.339***	0.403***	0.332***
Sum of lagged Net-Chargeoffs/Assets	-0.886***	-0.887***	-0.895***	-0.807***
$Liquid$	-0.880***	-0.699***	-1.907***	-0.879***
Sum of lagged $\Delta TED * Liquid$		-1.876***		-7.482***
Sum of lagged $\Delta TED * (1 - Liquid)$		0.662***		2.130***
Quart. Dummies	Yes	Yes	Yes	Yes
R^2	0.135	0.137	0.130	0.133
Observ.	107023	107023	107023	107023

Standard errors are in parentheses. *, **, *** denotes significance at 10%, 5% and 1% levels.

www.ingramcontent.com/pod-product-compliance
Lightning Source LLC
Chambersburg PA
CBHW081803170526
45167CB00008B/3304